IN THE GARDEN

David M. Schwartz *is an award-winning author of children's books, on a wide variety of topics, loved by children around the world.* Dwight Kuhn's *scientific expertise and artful eye work together with the camera to capture the awesome wonder of the natural world.*

For a free color catalog describing Gareth Stevens Publishing's list of high-quality books and multimedia programs, call 1-800-542-2595 (USA) or 1-800-461-9120 (Canada). Gareth Stevens Publishing's Fax: (414) 225-0377.

Library of Congress Cataloging-in-Publication Data

Schwartz, David M.
    In the garden / by David M. Schwartz; photographs by Dwight Kuhn.
       p. cm. — (Look once, look again)
    Includes bibliographical references (p. 23) and index.
    Summary: Explores the peas, potatoes, pumpkins, and other
vegetables in a garden, as well as the insects and other animals
that help them grow.
    ISBN 0-8368-2242-0 (lib. bdg.)
    1. Garden ecology—Juvenile literature. [1. Vegetables. 2. Gardens.
3. Garden animals. 4. Garden ecology. 5. Ecology.] I. Kuhn, Dwight, ill.
II. Title. III. Series: Schwartz, David M. Look once, look again.
QH541.5.G37S39 1998
577.5'54—dc21   98-6312

This North American edition first published in 1999 by
Gareth Stevens Publishing
1555 North RiverCenter Drive, Suite 201
Milwaukee, Wisconsin 53212 USA

First published in the United States in 1997 by Creative Teaching Press, Inc., P.O. Box 6017, Cypress, California, 90630-0017.

Text © 1997 by David M. Schwartz; photographs © 1997 by Dwight Kuhn. Additional end matter © 1999 by Gareth Stevens, Inc.

Printed in the United States of America

1 2 3 4 5 6 7 8 9 03 02 01 00 99

IN THE GARDEN

by David M. Schwartz

photographs by Dwight Kuhn

A SPRINGBOARDS INTO SCIENCE SERIES

Gareth Stevens Publishing
MILWAUKEE

This is called an eye, but it cannot see you! What has eyes, but cannot see?

A potato! A potato's eyes are actually buds. With water and sunlight, these buds sprout and grow into stems and leaves.

Some of the stems grow underground with the roots. They are called tubers. Tubers grow big and round — until we eat them!

Does this animal have a bad case of warts? These aren't warts. They are bumps on the rough skin of an animal that hops.

Toads eat insects that want to eat your garden. One toad can eat ten thousand insects in a summer. We should be friendly to toads!

If you get close enough,
it looks like a big green
balloon. It is green —
but not big! It is a green
vegetable as small as a …

9

...pea. The little round peas you eat are seeds. Peas form in pods.

When pea pods split open, the seeds can grow into new plants. If you eat the seeds first, they will help you grow!

What is wearing polka dots?
It is not a lady. It's a bug.

Ladybugs are beetles. Beetles have hard wing cases to protect their wings. The colorful wing cases warn birds that ladybugs taste terrible. Usually, birds leave them alone.

Ladybugs are welcome in a garden because they eat other insects.

Whose tiny seeds are these?
If you touch this bright red fruit, it feels a little rough.
But it tastes smooth and sweet.

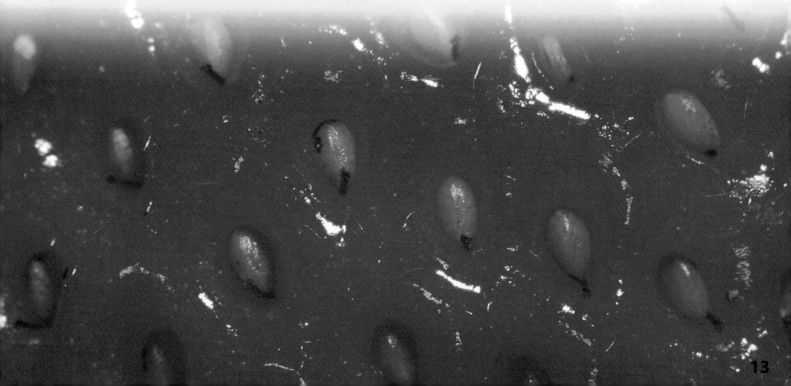

Strawberries are tasty treats. Animals like to eat them, too. They eat the berries and later spread their seeds. This is how strawberries grow in new places.

This leg is as sharp as a knife. It moves quickly. It grabs prey with deadly force. This leg belongs to …

...a praying mantis. The praying mantis is not really praying.
It is preying! The praying mantis eats many small insects in the garden.
In some places, it is against the law to kill a praying mantis.

Eat it or carve it.
Make it into a pie or a
jack-o'-lantern. What would
Halloween and autumn be
like without this plant?

17

Inside a pumpkin, you will find many seeds. The seeds grow into new pumpkins. Some pumpkins grow to more than 500 pounds (225 kilograms)!

For Halloween, people carve pumpkins into jack-o'-lanterns. For Thanksgiving, they bake pumpkin pies. Some people eat the seeds as a healthy, crunchy snack.

A.

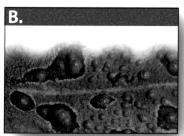

B.

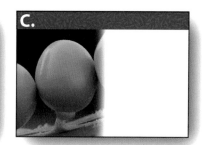

C.

D.

E.

F.

G.

Look closely. Can you name these plants and animals?

A.

Potatoes

B.

Toad

C.

Peas

D.

Ladybug

E.

Strawberries

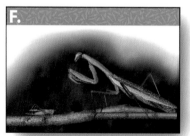

F.

Praying mantis

G.

Pumpkins

How many were you able to identify correctly?

bud: the small swelling on a branch or stem of a plant that contains a flower, shoot, or leaf that has not yet developed and opened.

carve: to cut, usually in a shape. Some people like to carve pumpkins at Halloween.

crunchy: a type of cracking or crushing sound.

eye: the bud of a potato plant. The buds are planted so they will sprout into new plants.

flash: a short, sudden burst of light.

force (n): strength; power.

healthy: not sick; having strength.

pod: a seed case for peas, beans, and some other plants. When ripe, the pod splits open to release the seeds.

praying mantis: a large insect related to grasshoppers that feeds on other insects. The praying mantis grasps its prey in its folded front legs.

prey: an animal hunted by another animal for food.

rough: bumpy or uneven; not smooth.

sprout: a young plant growth, like a bud or seedling.

tasty: having a pleasing flavor; delicious.

tuber: the thickened, usually underground stem of some plants, such as the potato. The enlarged end of the stem is eaten.

warn: to make aware of danger.

wart: a small, hard lump on the skin.

ACTIVITIES

Egg-citing Indoor Garden
Plant an eggshell garden to brighten a sunny windowsill in your house. Have an adult hard boil six eggs and carefully cut each egg in half using a sawing action. Scoop out the egg and put aside. Then, wash and dry the eggshells. Put some damp cotton balls into the bottom of each shell. Sprinkle garden cress seeds on the moist cotton balls, and place your eggshells in a sunny location. Keep the cotton damp, and in a few days the seeds will sprout. If you'd like, you can decorate the shells with felt-tip markers.

Potato Prints
Ask an adult to help you cut a potato in half. Use a felt-tip marker to draw a design on the part of the potato that does not have skin. Then, have the adult help you carefully cut around the design. Use a paintbrush to apply a thick layer of tempera paint to your design or carefully dip the potato into some paint. Press your potato stamp firmly onto a large piece of paper, then repeat in a different spot. After you are done decorating the paper, use it to wrap a gift.

Seed Jewelry
Remove the seeds from a melon or pumpkin and wash them. After they dry, ask an adult to make a hole through each seed with a needle. Color the seeds with felt-tip markers. After they dry, thread the seeds onto a piece of elastic thread long enough for a necklace or bracelet.

Roasted Pumpkin Seeds
Scoop the seeds out of a pumpkin and wash them to remove all the fibers. Spread the seeds on a cookie sheet and sprinkle them with salt. Bake at 350° Fahrenheit (180° Centigrade) for thirty minutes. Let them cool, and enjoy!

More Books to Read

Anna's Garden Songs. Mary Q. Steele (Greenwillow Books)

The Garden in Our Yard. Greg Henry Quinn (Scholastic)

In My Garden. Ron Maris (Greenwillow)

Ladybugs. Barrie Watts (Franklin Watts)

The Nature and Science of Seeds. Exploring the Science of Nature (series).
    Jane Burton and Kim Taylor (Gareth Stevens)

Walk a Green Path. Betsy Lewin (Lothrop, Lee & Shepard Books)

Videos

Get Ready...Get Set...Grow! (Cornell University)

Insects That Help Us. (Phoenix/BFA Films & Video)

The Praying Mantis. (Barr Films)

Web Sites

homeandfamily.com/gard.html

www.dole5aday.com/cool_stuff/potato/potato_grown.html

Some web sites stay current longer than others. For further web sites, use your search engines to locate the following topics: *garden, ladybug, potato, praying mantis, seeds,* and *tubers.*

INDEX